SCIENCE KIDS
Seasons

FALL

Aaron Carr

LET'S READ
AV²
BY WEIGL™
ADDED VALUE • AUDIO VISUAL

Go to **www.av2books.com**, and enter this book's unique code.

BOOK CODE

T646533

AV² by Weigl brings you media enhanced books that support active learning.

AV² provides enriched content that supplements and complements this book. Weigl's AV² books strive to create inspired learning and engage young minds in a total learning experience.

Your AV² Media Enhanced books come alive with...

Audio
Listen to sections of the book read aloud.

Video
Watch informative video clips.

Embedded Weblinks
Gain additional information for research.

Try This!
Complete activities and hands-on experiments.

Key Words
Study vocabulary, and complete a matching word activity.

Quizzes
Test your knowledge.

Slide Show
View images and captions, and prepare a presentation.

... and much, much more!

Published by AV² by Weigl
350 5th Avenue, 59th Floor
New York, NY 10118

Website: www.av2books.com   www.weigl.com

Library of Congress Control Number: 2013934643
ISBN 978-1-62127-491-9 (hardcover)
ISBN 978-1-62127-497-1 (softcover)

Printed in the United States of America in North Mankato, Minnesota
3 4 5 6 7 8 9 0   17 16 15 14

012014
WEP270114

Senior Editor: Aaron Carr
Art Director: Terry Paulhus

Weigl acknowledges Getty Images as the primary image supplier for this title.

SCIENCE KIDS
Seasons

FALL

CONTENTS

2   AV² Book Code
4   The Seasons
6   What is Fall?
8   Longest Night
10 Cool Weather
12 Ready for Winter
14 A New Coat
16 Moving with the Seasons
18 Changing Colors
20 Harvest Time
22 Fall Quiz
24 Key Words

There are four seasons in a year.
Fall is one of the seasons.
Fall is also called autumn.

4

Summer

Fall

Fall comes after summer and before winter.

Spring

Winter

5

6

Fall is a time of change.
Days become shorter
and nights become longer.

In parts of Alaska,
the Sun sets in November.
The Sun does not rise again
until January.

Weather begins to change
in the fall.
Warm summer weather
becomes cooler.

There is more rain in the fall
than in the summer.
It may even snow in the fall.

11

Fall is when animals get ready for the winter.
Some animals grow thicker fur to stay warm.

12

13

Some animals
change color in the fall.
This helps them
hide in the snow.

14

15

Some animals move
to a new home in the fall.
Humpback whales swim
thousands of miles
to find warmer waters in the fall.

Many birds fly to warmer places
in the fall.

Plants also change in the fall.
Fall is when leaves change colors.

Green leaves turn yellow, red,
orange, or brown in the fall.

18

19

Fall is when farmers pick fruits
and vegetables.
This is called the harvest.
Corn, apples, pumpkins, and turnips
are all picked in the fall.

The Moon may look
large and red in the fall.
This is called a harvest moon.

Fall Quiz

Test what you have learned about fall. Fall is all about changes. What changes do you see in these pictures?

23

KEY WORDS

Research has shown that as much as 65 percent of all written material published in English is made up of 300 words. These 300 words cannot be taught using pictures or learned by sounding them out. They must be recognized by sight. This book contains 61 common sight words to help young readers improve their reading fluency and comprehension. This book also teaches young readers several important content words, such as proper nouns. These words are paired with pictures to aid in learning and improve understanding.

Page	Sight Words First Appearance
4	a, also, are, four, in, is, of, one, the, there, year
5	after, and, before, comes
7	change, days, nights, time
8	again, does, not, parts, sets, until
10	even, it, may, more, than, to
12	animals, for, get, grow, some, when
14	helps, them, this
17	find, home, many, miles, move, new, places, waters
18	or, plants
21	all, large, look
22	about, do, have, pictures, see, these, what, you

Page	Content Words First Appearance
4	autumn, fall, seasons
5	spring, summer, winter
8	Alaska, January, November, Sun
10	rain, weather
12	fur
14	color, snow
17	birds, humpback whales
18	leaves
21	apples, corn, farmers, fruits, harvest, Moon, pumpkins, turnips, vegetables
22	quiz

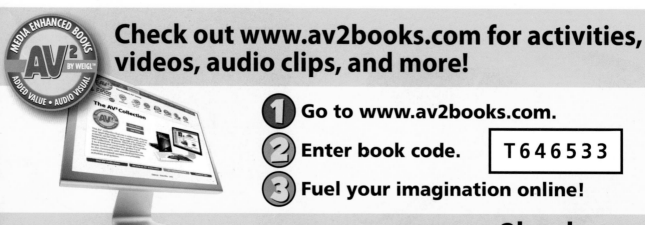

Check out www.av2books.com for activities, videos, audio clips, and more!

1 Go to www.av2books.com.

2 Enter book code. `T 6 4 6 5 3 3`

3 Fuel your imagination online!

www.av2books.com